## PRAISE FOR AÏCHA MARTINE THIAM

*AT SEA* is Aïcha Martine Thiam's sublime siren's song of the emerging self. The verse drifts dexterously from treading water, "a fish in your sea" to the triumphant thrash of the "pirate mermaid" who navigates and narrates her own divine depths.

— KRISTIN GARTH, AUTHOR OF *GIRLARIUM* AND EDITOR-IN-CHIEF OF *PINK PLASTIC HOUSE*

A heartfelt, humorous, open-ended discussion about what it means to be a Black woman in the world today. I felt so seen within the pages of *AT SEA*, that I oftentimes had to look through the pages to see if Thiam had dedicated this book to me. Wonderful. Just wonderful.

— KATHERINE D. MORGAN, ASSISTANT FEATURES EDITOR FOR *THE RUMPUS* AND AUTHOR OF *NO SELF-RESPECTING WOMAN*

Aïcha Martine rejects the cultural expectations that dictate what her story as a Black girl should be. In *AT SEA*, she tells her own coming-of-age story, unraveling trauma and exploring healing with all their nuance and complexity. *AT SEA* grapples with grief, disillusionment, and being forced to grow up too quickly and reaches for moments of childlike wonder. Aïcha Martine creates her own mythology complete with Bluebeard and mermaids and sailors. She fluidly slips between poetry and prose as she rewrites her story, imagining all the ways it could be. You can hear the rhythm and musicality of her poetry as lines echo into refrains, as she returns to a familiar line, only to twist it and imbue it with new meaning. Aïcha Martine finds liberty in her voice in *AT SEA*.

— CAROLINA VONKAMPEN, PUBLISHER AND EDITOR IN CHIEF OF *CAPSULE STORIES*

Dizzying, perplexing, delightful lines, brimming with glimpses from a nimble mind. I can't read these poems quickly. Can I take my time? I love, and I understand, how this poet leaps at us, arms wide ("Always, I get operatic."), and then retreats, self-doubting ("How can I trust the triteness of my senses?"). She's like your smartest, funniest, oddest friend, the one you always want more of, the one whose place you long to visit (too often? You'll bring wine), and sigh into her couch and ask her, again, "Will you show me what you're writing?"

— ELLEN PARKER, FOUNDER AND EDITOR-IN-CHIEF OF *FRIGG: A MAGAZINE OF FICTION AND POETRY*

*AT SEA* is a collection of poetry that explores the depth of grief, cultural identity, trauma and all of the emotions that come along with them. Just like a voyage on the ocean each page looms with magical moon — like wordcraft that pulls the tide. Some of these tides are contemplated in a slow rocking and others are tumultuous. Aïcha Martine Thiam uncovers the shipwrecks of sadness and despair with a deft hand and pulls us to the surface gasping for air. This book is a full fathom five into the sea change of human experience.

— JULIETTE VAN DER MOLEN, AUTHOR OF *DEATH LIBRARY, MOTHER, MAY I?, ANATOMY OF A DRESS* AND *CONFESS: THE UNTOLD STORY OF DOROTHY GOOD*

Aïcha Martine Thiam's *AT SEA* pulsates with a magnetic, mercurial energy at its center as it takes its own advice to "find your own language/make your grief sing". These poems shapeshift, often channelling the mythic and elemental as it deftly interrogates themes of womanhood, trauma and cultural inheritance. The speaker of *AT SEA* refuses to look away. She holds a bright fury in her hands, a desire for redress and still, hope. "Still yearning to be handled tenderly," this is a collection that urges the reader too to handle ourselves and each other with a little more tenderness. Here is a collection unafraid to cast us adrift in turbulent waters, but always with a promise to reel us back in.

— JIHYUN YUN, WINNER OF THE PRAIRIE SCHOONER BOOK PRIZE IN POETRY AND AUTHOR OF *SOME ARE ALWAYS HUNGRY*

In *AT SEA*, Martine uses repetition to examine the state of one's womanhood under patriarchy. In villanelles and pantoums, as well as other poetic forms, Martine approaches themes of grief and trauma through a succession of anhedonic refrains. At times reminiscent of Blake's *Visions of the Daughters of Albion*, the many voices in these poems echo the pain and longing of one another. Like the men Martine observes, she has "long understood the small workings of one's hatred for women" and demands of the reader, "Could/you live with yourself if you did not have your say?" By the end of *AT SEA*, your answer will certainly be no. By the end of *AT SEA*, "You, too, may one day want to fling up your heart like confetti."

— ISOBEL O'HARE, FOUNDING EDITOR OF *DREAM POP* AND AUTHOR OF *ALL THIS CAN BE YOURS*

To set adrift in the symphony of Aïcha Martine Thiam's poetry collection, *AT SEA*, is to wade into the personal mythology of irised terrains, passions, emotions, and perceptions of an agile, luminescent mind. Rapt with the desire for love, for life — from the prosaic to the sacred — Thiam radiates deep knowing and resonance. Exploring the joys and anguish of being a woman of color in a world that habitually exiles and others, the speaker discerns: "Brown girl: you don't get a plot twist." And yet these exquisite poems keep searching, building, transcending, like the tide — seeking some measure of justice, some grace — for the soul defies rote delineations. "Heart lies in the dented hollow of my lung, skin/of solitude swathes the body like a sheet, and/I cherish the steady cadence of my bone," there is rapturous might in these pages.

— SU HWANG, RECIPIENT OF THE MINNESOTA
BOOK AWARDS IN POETRY AND AUTHOR OF *BODEGA*

# AT SEA

## AÏCHA MARTINE THIAM

# CL◀SH

Copyright © 2021 by Aïcha Martine Thiam

Cover by Joel Amat Güell

joelamatguell.com

CLASH Books

Troy, NY

clashbooks.com

All rights reserved.

No part of this book may be reproduced in any form or by any electronic or mechanical means, including information storage and retrieval systems, without written permission from the author, except for the use of brief quotations in a book review.

This book is a work of fiction. Names, characters, businesses, places, incidents and events are either the products of the author's imagination or used in a fictitious manner. Any resemblance to actual persons, living or dead, or actual events is purely coincidental.

## CONTENTS

| | |
|---|---:|
| I.   HELLO, SAILOR! | 1 |
| Icarus Bystander | 2 |
| And You Will Call Me Bluebeard | 4 |
| Bald Eyes | 11 |
| Succors | 13 |
| Very Specific Phobias | 15 |
| In-Out | 18 |
| Late Bloomer | 20 |
| Fortune Favors | 23 |
| Iotas | 25 |
| Hammers | 28 |
| | |
| II.   DRIFTER MERMAID | 31 |
| Hills to Die On | 32 |
| I Have Faith In Birds | 35 |
| The Thrill | 38 |
| Kintsugi of Sorts | 39 |
| So You've Got a Dinner Party | 41 |
| Inside Voices | 43 |
| Long Simmer | 51 |
| How Does She Talk? | 54 |
| Red and White Don't Run Together | 56 |
| Falderal | 59 |
| | |
| III.   HOLD THE WAVE | 62 |
| Holding Water | 63 |
| Echoes, Afterthoughts | 64 |
| Anhedonis, Anhedonia | 65 |
| Hothouse Flower | 67 |
| Paper Tiger Man | 69 |
| I Took A Stroll While Coming Down Undercloud | 72 |
| All This Mess, It Doesn't Leave You When You Go | 74 |
| Sometimes You Get The Bear | 76 |
| How You Write A Tall Tale | 79 |
| | 82 |

| | |
|---|---|
| Acknowledgments | 85 |
| About the Author | 87 |
| Also by CLASH Books | 89 |

# AT SEA

# I. HELLO, SAILOR!

## ICARUS BYSTANDER

I call people, listen to them talk
contribute nothing, hear them asking
how my day has been, how goes it all
and I contribute nothing. I would
much rather hear them talk over me
want to be walls people can step on
want to be cracks people don't sidestep
want to be windows barely glanced at
so I call and contribute nothing

I feel safe talking to drunk people
who won't remember what I tell them
days and days after it has all passed
I can unveil the chapters of my
dysfunction, and they will read them out
page by page like children, excited
to be offered a book of their own
be it one they barely understand
they coo and slur, and I indulge them

People with interesting stories
spill out, out over the rest of us
they make us question all our morals
what we wouldn't do to get a taste

of that old "I, too, have been, have seen"
they render us anxious and ashamed
as much as they, too, fascinate us
what I wish I feasted on: hope, love
I heave out instead that muted hush

## AND YOU WILL CALL ME BLUEBEARD

You would be wrong
Thinking I have fled you
Thinking you have fled me
It is the unpressed nucleus
The unuttered understanding
The auguries that spell perditions
And deliverances.
You would be wrong
When my present is multitudes
Knotting with your pasts
You would be wrong
And that is not all.

I've lived in small spaces all my life
Lifetimes and avenues
Walked with you
My existence splintered where it meets yours
We have lived the grandest of lives
Been people, and then been others
Had others
We have gone and come again
Existences poked and prodded through the Needles
Of time
Dying when the other pulls through

Living together, sometimes apart
Sometimes never meeting.
Nine lives to match the cats
We always wished we could be.

In one lifetime,
My heart is sixteen years old
And yours is ancient, callous, cold
I give you everything
And you don't trust me
This is the story of how I write books to make you forgive
And you, you look for lines so you can read between them.

There is another one, where I am graceless
But you are unconcerned about it
We bond over music and green tea
And exchange fervent recommendations
That border on the aggressive
So that it makes me smile
That passion of yours suffusing every title
And the rich tartness in the tea
And you cannot wait, and I can't contain it
And sometimes, I even think I may
I may
I might
Love you.

That is not all, that is not it.

In another, I break your heart so many times you
Come to expect it, like the end of a calamitous song
We see each other this way and that
Cocking our expectations
Slanting our heads
Angling our gazes
Clinging onto the airless center like it's a ball of light
Which we will never figure out
And it is probably for the best.

Here I peer another tangent
Ever so slight, ever so parallel
But it makes all the difference
Because where you once loved me
Now it is the other way around
And I am unmoved by it.
I feel old.

That is not all, that is not all.

I spy another
But this one is dim, dull, bleak
We are grieving for bygones, lovers lost
Superimposing their souls onto each other
Disappointed when the likeness does not assuage
The shattered heart
And what could have been never is
Which does not matter because I am but a drop of ink in your water
And you are a thumb of graphite, streaked on the side of my page
I do not, cannot care
And it soothes me when you likewise don't.
This one should have been left alone.

Here a version, where
Nothing is funny, and everything's a joke
My sense of humor sours and you take to appraising
and assassinating
My character with hilarious, devastating takedowns
I will drive off with the last word,
Dashing away at your fragile ego
With a witty, well placed observation on your tragic upbringing
And it will make you smile even as you excoriate
My name.

And that is not all, not all.

Life number sixteen:
You leave me
But I keep your books

And every now and then
I smell them to remind me of
You.
When you ask for them, the lie skates smoothly down my tongue
I tell you I've already given them
Away, sold them
Palming coins to illustrate my point.

My favorite cycle is also my worst
Kindling my masochism because it's the only thing I cherish more than you
In it, you struggle with some secret pain
But you leave me out of it
And so I begin to do the same.
But years later you will say that I was the one, pushed you out
The way I pushed out snow, caked up on the sills of our apartment window.

There will be another time,
When Chance, munificent Chance will
Chance a glance on us again.
Your mother will try to hate me, but I am a paragon
Your careless father will pretend he doesn't care, but I am Beguilement Itself
Your brother will wish that I had chosen him instead.
I end up bowed over you
And we make deathbed promises
Sated with the fruits of our rapture.

But that is not it.

It's not yet the one I think of
Not the one I'll think of years later
When I cross paths with you, a stranger one summer morning
Caught between two errands
You will stun me
Then and there
And I will not know your name
But I will never forget you

Forget the children I imagine for me and you
Forget the tangles we could make together
Forget the potential that fades as soon as you exit my periphery
Taking the clarity with me
You will break my heart, you whose name I will never learn (though I will certainly speculate)
But you will also save my life
Because I will look to the future as the softest place to fall
As long as it holds the promise that another summer morning may come
Where you and I will meet again.

In some separate continuance, your insecurities bend with my callowness
You, a seasoned cynic
I: have never been kissed
This is what you know: that I would endure it all for anyone
This is what I don't: that your kindness, dangled under your contempt, will break me.

(And I don't think some of you boys understand
The power that you have

How you can undo a girl with a barbed wire of a word
Dragged gently across her heart

It is casual
And all the more punishing for it

Casual and clever
In a clueless, guileless way
A guileless sort of way

— but I was saying. That is not yet the point.)

In the semantics of our lives, one sliver of me
Will meet your wholeness
And you will try to complement me
And I go mad thinking you will save me
When I should know better by now
Being a liver of life

And an inveterate reader of ghastly fairy tales
Whose morbid true versions
Hold nothing to their shiny counterparts
A lie
I'm eager to believe in, because
You do.

Here, a pitiful glimpse
You are the white noise I let whisper in the background
The simmering television screen I leave on for comfort
The tuneless music I dial up for company
The brouhaha that steels my loneliness
And why do I keep thinking we're Saturday?
And why am I watching this again?

There, a sweeter one
Take a breath, I'll take one too
I'll make you like bowling again, might even tolerate mini golf
Peel off those tepid, tarnished memories you have of pointless sports
And we'll sate ourselves on promises
We don't dare yet speak aloud
For fear of what, of what.

And that is not all, not yet.

This one stream runs completely separate
And ever more troubling for it
We end up together
Accidentally
Sit on bar tables in crowded restaurants
Footnotes in each other's lives
Scattered for the sake of others
If we both looked up, we could read eternity in each other
But you don't like eye contact, and besides
I only wear shades.

Another one finds me the victim
Of your rancor, long fingers reaching from past experiences
Caressing warnings for you, that

Only you can sense.
They echo: *she is dangerous*
And you will treat me as such
Realizations, barred and nettled
Tightrope dancing
Over imagined foreboding.

In one story, you get comfortable too quickly
You call me "baby", which chafes, but also somehow doesn't
You speak low over the music, so that I have to get closer to hear you
And it works.

You would be wrong
Thinking I have fled you as you are
When we are fleeing everything we could be

And that is not all:
Like clockwork, our treads hammering the face
Our needles chase after one another
Chiming about regrets, about lifetimes and avenues
Of treachery and reverence
I dance away your mangled heart with glee
Because I can
And you will hate me (there are too many versions where you hate me)
Even as you double back
Six times you will lose, in order:
Your essence
Your poise
Your hopefulness
Your idealism
Your will, that vital urgency to live
Your — I might stop there.
And you will call me Bluebeard
A thief and murderer after your own lapidated heart

And of all there is, that might be all.

## BALD EYES


i like cities that do not sleep
washed out throughfares shadow us with bald eyes
leveled sidewalks, elation in inflorescence
because i like cities that do not sleep
and if my chaos were an ingot
i'd make enough to rattle the world's indifference
love cities that do not sleep
washed out throughfares shadow me with bald eyes

noctivagance is a peril, insomnia is a gift
inculcate those truths as much as conscience will allow me
douse myself in them as i walk, muscles taut as a promise
"noctivagance is a peril, insomnia is a gift"
at bay, at bay, all else this sidewalk-flattening produces
and if my chaos were an ingot, i would trust that
noctivagance is a peril, insomnia is a gift
inculcate those truths as much as conscience will allow me

those washed out throughfares shadow me with bald eyes
at bay, at bay, all else this sidewalk-flattening produces
i walked until the pinched nerve in my ribcage released with a sigh
washed out throughfares shadow with a bald eye
i walked until i ground my notions of home to a powdery dust

until even noctivagance itself, no longer wonder traded for, at bay
until the washed out throughfare itself closed its balding eyes
and all that sidewalk-flattening made of my insomnia a farce

# SUCCORS

There is a kettle-shaped hole
where my heart used to be
a hole in the kettle
just small enough for water
to seep where it should not
a hole so small as to be overlooked
but not small enough
that the kettle, my kettle
could keep soldiering on.

It is ugly, it is worn
dull silver
but here and there flecked
with hearty browns and lively coppers.

It is rugged, weathered
tiptoeing on obsolete
but never one to leave in the lurch
now I am left in a state.

Sometimes cast amid
the dirty dishes
that tend to pile up on
an overwhelmed gal

if it had a mouth
it would probably say
it had been mistreated
and I don't quite deserve
to justify myself.

Like a friend
who will never say no
I became reliant
on the helping hand
the palm ever outstretched
and that friend, it was worn
rather than broken
testifying to the times
my life has hinged on what came pouring from that rusted spout.

A cup of tea on a rainy day, a cup of tea with a book.
A cup of tea before bed, a cup of tea to wake a tired body up.
A cup of tea to nurse blistered fingers, a cup of tea to un-furrow a lowly brow.
A cup of tea to distract, a cup of tea for something to do.
A cup of tea to bring a manic girl down, a cup of tea to dizzy up a soul.
A cup of tea because it's there, a cup of tea because why not.
A cup of tea so as not to eat, a cup of tea to distract a starving stomach.
A cup of tea to feel again, a cup of tea to warm thoughts gone cold.
A cup of tea for the burn of it, a cup of tea to press on and blister the skin.
A cup of tea to while away the wailing hour

a cup of tea to while away the tick-ticking of a lonely heart.

## VERY SPECIFIC PHOBIAS

We used to talk,
we used to have conversations big
and Small.
But really, they were never small.
Never felt small.
It's not the same.
Time was like cotton candy,
sugar tendrils we could twist
and Pull
to our whims and fancies;
and even when our fingers would
bind together, and there was that
paranoia about the bugs
(there was always that paranoia about the bugs — it was summer,
and we had very specific phobias)
it was always so very sweet.
Wasn't it always so very sweet?
I wouldn't know.
I've stopped remembering.
The words slip-staggered, somewhere along the way
between:
my constricted throat
and the air, thick with
saids and unsaids

which could not sustain them;
somewhere along the way
between
my thinking that they had the power to change you
and my realizing that they didn't;
and somewhere along the way
between
what I thought I knew, and
what I wish someone had told me.
I've traded those words, like I've traded everything else.
Sensations beg for my attention nowadays
and I, I look for some sense in them.
I get the hankering.
I feel the storm.
I turn blue.
Always, I get operatic.
Fling me over rocks
where the heartbroken sea comes to die;
dangle me over precipices
where I may find those aforementioned
words,
lost so very long ago.
It's not the same.
It's not the same.
I chased those sweet, sticky days
down acrid, dusty roads.
I looked for your rainbow tinged shadow
through warped lenses, broken perspectives;
I broke my skin, walking over our
sharded-yet-still-riveting past.
It's not the same.
Won't ever likely be.
I've lost count of lost sleep.
Settled like dust on my own disgraces.
Made a different peace. But
I still feel small,
sometimes.
Time will no longer accommodate:
She has other children to coddle,

and children we are no longer.
I still have very specific phobias.
I often wonder about yours, too.
We used to talk,
so I wouldn't know.

## IN-OUT

When I do the old in-out in-out, my throat is mine to hold,
fingers hug the lip of the sink, tumble, tumble, down it goes.
But the question, like my pounding blood, insists: when do I know I'm finished?
I never seem to find the end,
like a depth-less pit, a tale with no conclusion —
except this tale is of my own making, an endeavor I must finish one way or another,
if not here and now, then a road no less difficult, in fact more.
By the razor, by the line, by the abstinence, by the nail, the voices, and I come back to the tumbling,
sometimes.
Despite the hum and the sigh of my aching body,
I find I leave the job unfinished. Might I as well have never started?
Would it make a difference, asks my disappointed conscience? It would not, if not for the present, ever painful pull
on the side of my throat.
Days later, it will remind me that indeed I did,
and I was there at that time, and the sink remembers,
and my throat remembers,
and my lungs remember,
and my stomach, the muscles they do remember,
and my heart, soldiering on,
it does remember, remember it does.

I don't forget.
And when I step back just to come back to it again,
In a few hours' days' months' or weeks' time,
I return to the dance,
I un-pause the melody
and reclaim this rhythm I know so well,
know so well.

## LATE BLOOMER

These things add up,
but if you sparse them out, spread them like spilled salt,
you could trick the eye,
the ever vigilant Eye.

I want to be twenty-seven
the only way left is down.
I could be a woman at last
torture myself with earn-ed, willful skill.
Could learn to love myself one day, or else choose
not to.
Wouldn't matter, I'd be free at last,
free to scorn, free at last.

These things add up.
Escape so much you end up on trajectories of fugue,
hoping momentum will buoy you where accountability did not.

I want to have the star treatment,
the right to blow hysterics and own my titular mess, holy mess,
holiness.
I want to be pampered
the way women who have stopped caring are warranted:
what particular favors do I need to turn in?

These things sure do add up.
Or maybe the times have changed.
Maybe my times have changed:
I want an honorary degree.

Go into slow sentences, big words, long stories, always have the last say.
I've gotten older, but —
realizing I'm nothing but a parentheses, I've been on a tangent since
— I want to be twenty-seven, that age that might anchor me,
the way twenty-three
and
twenty-five
did not.

It's that floating, that eternal floating.
These things add up, you see.
It's that infernal sound again, the sound of your conscience gone hollow,
gone slippery,
gone bright,
your fingers struggle around its form, its shape, its contours.

It's stepping onto the patchy grass
and thinking you're still a child, your bones enveloped and protected by
the fleshiness of your idealism.
It's stepping into thorns of potential sufferings
(in the form of poison ivy and other hostile flora)
and thinking yourself made of leather and hide —

no.
It's stepping onto a trampoline
thinking fun will be had, for the very last time
and for the very last time, feeling like God Herself leant over you and
made you Sovereign.

These things add up
they add up
and I could never really count them.
I was terrible with numbers,
still am.

21

They jeer and needle me and I can only offer pallid retorts.
So I step on the trampoline instead
because I won't feel like a fool, even if I am
because I haven't earned the right to want more.
I am not twenty seven.

I know my time is coming
so I go to meet with it instead
twirling like I am still made of feathers
not stones.
Like my youthful charm will last forever.
Hopingprayingwishing
the trampoline won't let me down
and giving guarantees I cannot follow through.

Because these things add up,
and before you know it you are spent,
playing Faustian games with yourself
whose consequences won't matter, as long as the
trampoline won't let you down.
It's that floating, that floating you swim to
as long as the
trampoline won't let you down.
It's that trance you throw your entire body into, pleading
that the trampoline
won't let you down
won't let you down.

## FORTUNE FAVORS

I had just begun looking down that winding road
        to fathom its edges, serpentine and deceitful
I knew their sorrow for what it was, the women in my family
        but others would call it ill-temper
Brown girl: you don't get a plot twist. Your story's been penned
        with strokes as hollow as they are spiteful

Sorrow, stripped of its subtlety, the darker the shade swathing our skins
        a notion too vague to center
My mother's anguish dismissed as commonplace anger
        I squinted at that winding road, saw what it tried to tell me
I knew their sorrow for what it was, the women in my family
        but others would call it ill-temper
Brown girls don't go crazy: colorful props in others' catastrophes
        is all we'll ever get to be
This complexity you feast on in pages, songs and film
        you were never meant to carry this
My mother's anguish dismissed as commonplace anger
        I squinted at that winding road, saw what it tried to tell me

We are allowed to peek it, call it even by name
        but cannot gaze into the fabled Abyss
You, too, may one day want to fling up your heart like confetti

        but you don't get a coming-of-age
This complexity you feast on in pages, songs and film
        you were never meant to carry this

Only wisdom, biting wisdom, wisdom enough to grasp
        the sublime nuances of rage
Throw away that slice-of-life caprice and those thoughtful narratives

        the world has other things in store
You, too, may one day want to fling up your heart like confetti
        but you don't get a coming-of-age

Throw away that slice-of-life caprice and those thoughtful narratives

        the world has other things in store
Though I had just begun looking down that winding road
        to fathom its edges, serpentine and deceitful
Girl, you will gash your fingers on the prick of anonymity
        and never dare ask for more
You don't get a plot twist. Your story's been penned
        with strokes as hollow as they are spiteful

# IOTAS

The earliest memory I have of seeing wonder in liminal spaces
is the Lac Rose in Senegal, a fairytale pond, and I am a fairytale princess
pirate mermaid in a pixie dust soup
spent my childhood in a mythology of sorts
halfway between the color and the puckered mouth that always tried to suction it away

I was three when the Dakar deluge brought an avalanche of ants in its wake
the first I ever touched on terror, a phobia that would latch onto me forever
not the rain — the rain I loved from the moment it sprayed my arid soul
— but the ants
swarm of fitful frenzy in my grandmother's garden
taught me how easily chaos could upset comfort

But that's not all I remember
just as they streamed around me: floating
swept in my uncle's solid arms
we became an island in the middle of the crawling storm
and just as I had known fear, I knew what love was

Even when years later a cloud of locusts descended upon Nouakchott
and ate through everything

sunlight crisscrossed, the air a click-click of wings
and snapping pinchers
it felt prophetic, biblical, formidable in its scale

> Later, in different cities, we would try to replicate the feeling of being protagonists in a magical realism season, and although it came close, was never really close; Arctic Monkeys and golden colored hues in Chicago; streetlamps that pulled the focus onto blue moon territory in Washington DC; in Libreville, freckled wetness dappling the sound of the world; Paris bringing with its scent of blossoms a lyricism from another time; Nairobi and its multitudinous textures, like running fingers through multiverses

> In Montréal we almost made it, losing hours in the darkened rooms of the Dollar Cinema place that smelled of vinegar and feet, watching films we didn't care for but felt we had to, because they were essentially free and we could afford it, enduring one too many found footage plots and letting tolerance run its course, and knowing we deserved more, but bonding over the shared ridiculousness of this patchwork kind of fun

When I think of childhood I think of
all the times I got lost in old mattress stores in Maryland
believing we would die during Y2K and relishing the thrill
reading Archie comics and responding to Veronica, but pretending I was a Betty
wandering in the labyrinthine halls of the Jeepers arcade
quiet summer shades, caterpillars curled around my index
fevered days off from school, watching science documentaries under covers
splitting hairs between Baby Spice and Sporty Spice but really feeling Scary
rice pudding, power outages by the living room fire
Christmas lights and snow in the twilight in Virginia
shredded gift wrappings wreathed around poking toes in socks
life changing crises that could only paralyze a seven year old

> But it never comes close to when I was this high, and I could barely reach the tabletops, inhaling the ample heat of the West African monsoon; not close enough to the tang of the Madd and Toll seeds, as sour as they were

sweet, the roasting peanuts on coals and sand; kneeling by my grandmother's feet as she sent for beignets and seared corn cobs from passing vendors. It never comes close to seeing my mother be a daughter, see her gently chided by her uncles, to watching telenovelas with my cousins until the sun came up, to lying on woven matting and simmering peppermint candies in buttermilk in Rosso, to watching B-list 80's action films my aunt always took too seriously

When my grandmother died I knew
iota by iota I would liquefy and ebb apart
until I was wave upon wave
and so I did, wrapped around myself with folk rock in my ear
until weeks became weeks upon weeks
and time lost track of me, little pebble in seabed
it does not matter, in the end, which version of childhood I hold true
my grandmother died, taking with her all my definitions of mirth
I was no longer a child by then
but always found it cruel that I couldn't pretend anymore
nonetheless

## HAMMERS

I know the taste of Regret all too well.
It chases down my throat after
saccharine Anxiety
and the bowled, bold, rounded
sourness of Depression
have had their say.

You begin to believe in the truths, the truths that aren't really truths
those false friends who sell you things you cannot afford
but which you would buy and believe nonetheless.
Those who whisper in the inky night
who sing your heart to sleep
and tell you:

that sadness is a state, not a transitory feeling
which will nail you to your cross
hour after day after year
while you wither and fill yourself
with cobwebs and failures
and the husk of broken promises.

That your are made of 'in's and 'un's:
In:
capable/nept/visible/curable

Un:
lovable/worthy/wanted.

That you deserve this, and that it could be worse.
It should be worse.
After all, you have not earned your peace
and you will sleep when
and only when you are dead
if you are so lucky.

That you may walk until you blister your soles
feel the tendrils of the hopeful wind
and you may even see the light and stretch out your hand
for it.
But you will never reach the end of this, whatever
this
is.

## II. DRIFTER MERMAID

## HILLS TO DIE ON

By contrast, they looked brave, the two women facing the drunk passersby
Who would not take back the casual abuse lathered from their leering mouths
Enraged, the women stood rooted on the sidewalk, shouting down their own instincts to fall back
And I thought: *that amour-propre, that love of oneself, where has mine dispersed*
Yes, I would have stirred, could have added to the refrain, should have led the charge
But dust weighed my grit to a halt. My heart was dead, I loved nothing, least of all myself

Sometimes I think: these slow burns, they are thankless; the world twists and leaves you
Baffled where you stand. Teeth grind as you take your thought vacations
And anesthetize your most vivacious impulses. I have done that letting go, that dutiful letting go
While I am thumbed like a slab of viscous meat by rugged, undeserving hands
Sometimes I think: one day my shrill heart will make you judder: but 'tis slow, and 'tis thankless
By contrast, they look brave, those women who face off with drunk passersby

The wind bit and pinched at me, on that icy sidewalk. The two women's voices
Marrying into that most formidable roar, silencing the catcalls
I used to be just as spirited, just as ablaze with indignation: these days I am —
The thought a heinous one I never want to carry to its end —
Just jaded. In the face of brutes whose pincers harass the wounds they've made
Who never take back the leering abuse lathered from their casual mouths

The wind bit and pinched at me like fingers and eyes have done so many times
Right then it occurred: these two, maybe they are new at this thing, this woman-ing woman-ness
They have not yet felt their hope deflate and die in their hearts owing to a
Trauma or two, expertly aimed their way. Perhaps they have not yet lost their footing
Over innocuous hurts: or worst of all, they are just not jaded yet
Enraged, they stood rooted on the sidewalk, shouting down their own instincts to just *let it go*

I bent away to another time in place, younger, yet so much less narrow
When certainty was an afterthought of strength: or perhaps was it arrogance all along
I collected them like dinted trophies, those insults, because they were my vindication
A point of pride — *you look like a bitch, why won't you crack a smile* —
Because it meant I had favored principle over Jaded, that dawning Jaded
And I hummed: *that amour-propre, that love of oneself, where has mine fucked off to*

Alternating between distress and disdain but with grace, always the grace
Seer of the souls, I have long understood the small workings of one's hatred for women
But that impulse to look beyond the ugliness of the offense, it is depleted
It's those words — *I forgive* — which I cannot say because the *give*

It does not sit well with me, not when all else has been given away
Still, I watched my sisters and I thought: *could have stirred, could have added to the refrain*

Girl, you are too old to be this dishonest. This, here, is where your ego goes to die
This is the place where your aspirations sour like forgotten cream
On sidewalks where hideous realizations are made and dull epiphanies are had
Where you confront your nesting-doll emotions and your infinite faithlessness
Where you watch women you could have been, could still be, do what *jaded* has robbed you of
It is known, and it feels right: my heart is dead, and I love nothing, least of all, myself.

# I HAVE FAITH IN BIRDS

i.

I'm good at cooking apology meals
People tend to falter before a feast
Where one has clearly labored
Put in sores and blood, put in even calluses
It doesn't do well to thrust rancor against grace
Doesn't look good on the wearer of that sentiment
I should know, been cooking a lot of these lately
And watching with knitted zest as they wrestled with
Whatever still compelled them to be forgiving
And gracious
Patient
And understanding
Sometimes it takes a bit longer, so
I think — despite knowing that I should not think this —
*Perhaps I should show them my scarred skin*
Pretend I knifed myself slicing radishes
Into juliennes
Pretend I'll endure anything for them with the proviso
That I be forgiven for things passed and yet to come
Nevermind that there were two lies in those sentences

ii.

I'm good with the plucking, with the feathers hurled like shrapnel
My own stories leave me cold
Impersonal as the hairs I meticulously yank from my body
Mine, but only temporarily so
Panoply of disjunction
I'm good with that strip and flaying
It's what comes after that I much less subscribe to
I carried evil eye jewelry for years
For fear I might attract more gazes
Than I knew what to do with
Look at me - don't look at me
See me - don't see me
Accusative.
The spleen impulse a systole
Beached and blanched
But still yearning to be handled tenderly
When I was a child I jitterbugged by myself in the middle of a roomful of adults
Even as I broke sweat over it, the weight of their eyes
I thought: eventually I'll take flight and all this will be just a memory
Worth the enduring of those fragile seconds of being seen

iii.

Today I thought I'd make an omelette
And the lid of the salt shaker tipped over and fell
A dull thud, a shower of salt like gentle spooling lace
My Father he doesn't like salt
My Mother, she doesn't mind
I idle at the stove thinking about balance beams and compromises
Thinking about waste and opportunity
I'm good when it comes to the begging-that-is-not-begging
Start with: making them think they are the ones at fault
I have never asked someone to stay
Have never asked someone to love me
Have never begged not to be left alone
At least not in so many words
I'd sooner warble to death
Eggshells are eggshells

So what if we crunch and step into them from time to time
Maybe that's why birds love me
And I love them (although they also terrify)
Because we both know the value of weightlessness
And of keeping wind underfoot

# THE THRILL

Hands are blossomed open, like vulgar vines
Like elongated petals, finger flowers, palm of patterns
Water hits like a salve, blurs their contours
And that is how I like it, is how it should be

Like elongated petals, finger flowers, palm of patterns
I should feel should be fine should be lucky should be fine
And that is how I like it, is how it should be
I am alive I am alive I am alive, alive, I, I am alive

I should feel should be fine should be lucky should be fine
Nothing does it, nothing ever does, nothing ever will
I am alive I am alive I am alive, alive, I, I am alive
Water graces aching skin, yet never more a part of me

Nothing does it, nothing ever does, nothing ever will
It does not sink in like it should, the thrill, live wire
Water graces aching skin, yet never more a part of me
Errant word wandering notion stray thought, and I begin to fray

# KINTSUGI OF SORTS

When people want to give me things, I say no thanks
I can handle nor the toll, nor the returns

Instead I say here you go, you take this instead
Forever in deficit, but I'll never be in debt

Little sister hollers in delight when she sees me
My people, they tell me they love me from time to time

Skipped record, I swerve over that sentiment
Why can't I have that same enthusiasm for people

I have to talk slow, keep those currents pulled inward
Because my voice it always totters toward the end

White-knuckle, flinch/flinch, need it kept at bay
Or else I'll signal failure like a Doppler effect

Draw nearer and it sounds shriller, distorted
But from afar, my cracks are dusted golden and they gleam

Magazine says they want to publish my words
Fellow artist tells me I am gifted

And I think they must not have any good taste
They must not have heard the waves

I should be a vacuum, charcoal and void-hollow
So that my soul-draining ways be at least justified

# SO YOU'VE GOT A DINNER PARTY

Do you split yourself, keep her at arm's length?
It's the only way to do it so you don't feel like
scream screaming. A scam, a scam, all of it
(although you've done a good job of playacting).
So you have accepted another dinner invitation
where you will slink and slink colorful around
others, as if to say *in all its glory, this is it
nothing else to see here*. They will lap it all up —
hell: you might even too. A scam, a scam, a scam.

And truly, I can only laugh.

I've seen the milk of the moon thaw into the water sky
have seen starlight work its way into the sootiest
corners of my soul. Oh do I know, it is a thing that exists.
Beautiful. Even as I dissipate my definitions of beauty,
I know that it is beautiful. So I try it on myself:
*You look fine, you look absolutely fine*
She rebuts: *revolting, don't you dare step outside.
Don't you know better by now? Why did you think
you were the moon?* No that's not right, you did not.

So really, I can only laugh.

Carve into your arm again to stop yourself from screaming;
Scam, scam, all of it. Split yourself, and by all means
go to the damn dinner already. Stop asking the permission,
you are the one stepping into your shoes,
she no longer has a say (although she has more to say than you).
Convince yourself the body you are looking at is not yours
because you have split yourself, although she is more you than you.
Brace yourself for your friends, for eating disorders as
cheap fodder, for would-be edgy dinnertime conversation.

Just laugh it off, if that is all you can do.

Yet: how can I trust these eyes when I have seen
the milk of the moon melt into the water sky
and take the shape of the mellowest pond?
In it I cast the debris of my convictions
and hope they simmer in that moonlight and those stars
and hope that when they come back to me
I, too, will be made of constellation cinders and luminescence.
How can I trust the triteness of my senses?
They rest on place cards with my name — no, her name — all over them.

And laugh, laugh, I can only laugh it off.

Fine, bring her along, pretend you are both normal, then;
when you laugh she'll try her best too,
emulating the pull of your muscles, the arch of your neck,
grinning, howling, screeching with abandon
as you both fondle the flab around your belly;
caress the creases and dips on your thighs;
paw at the thickness underneath your bra;
and keep it together, keep it together, get a grip,
even as you plead with her *work with me here*.

And laugh, laugh, laugh, no really please, just laugh it off.

# INSIDE VOICES

*Golden shovel after Sylvia Plath, "Lady Lazarus"*

i.

Those effigies I cannot keep, I peel;
gather the curlicues from the floor, dust off;
hunkered like the
rapacious guest who gathers the crumb in the napkin.

They tell me not to praise the feeling ("do not goad it") but, O
Greed, Holy Greed, my
composure has, on the contrary, been my enemy.
What more damage could this one matter do?

"Nurture the elegance," they say: I
lap up, instead, the ungainliness that does not terrify.
"Nurture the temperance, and
you will feast on *sang-froid* forever": I
rollick in that hideousness instead, a
hideousness that leaves my neuroses smiling.
I am more my woman
than the one you would make of me, of I.

My religion is that which hoards, destroys. I am

a follower of that which ravages, and ravages only.
I die at the altar of the rancor multiplied by ten, by thirty,
the malice and the mirth that chase with the question: yes? and?

If it can fill me, I will have it. I like
only that which howls back at the
doubt I cannot silence. Curiosity, and I am the cat
who flees where escape will take her: I

will not nurture said elegance. I will have
nine —
no, tenfold — the occasion, in other lifetimes, to roll with the times.
Meantime, I want only to

hurry, to wolf, to gather, to die.

ii.

Ah, freedom from the obligation, what
I wouldn't give. A
stream; from parted lips, a million
senseless words, tumbling like filaments.

Scatter them! They will tussle over it, the
insatiable exhibitionists, peanut-crunching
their right to emote, like crooners with a crowd.
I much prefer the quiet that sometimes rests, sometimes shoves.

I much prefer the solitude that sometimes does me in.
I much prefer Beaudelaire's spleen to
Keats' silver pinions, that summer bird I cannot see
that taunts and taunts my albatross. These

words I'd cast off, like the breadcrumbs they are;
let those, eager for a voice, have my
wasted spirit, have it all. These hands
will do my talking, these eyes will do my

pleading. Yes, the torsion will bring me to my knees.

But crooners beware: you're no better than I.
My voice promises me liberty — be that as it may,
I much prefer the lowly vapors when they let me be.

Heart lies in the dented hollow of my lung, skin
of solitude swathes the body like a sheet, and
I cherish the steady cadence of my bone.

iii.

Occupational hazard. Dying,
for the price of walking in one's open truth, is
a succession of copper-tinted bruises, an
exercise in the art
of endurance. I rip the pearls away, like
casting the lid off of everything
that propriety tells me I should hush — or else.

This wrath I engage in, I
nurse it like the sickish child left in the dust of its siblings. Do
up the quilts around it,
let it harbor and suckle on my lifeblood. Exceptionally,
I get Rockwellesque: rage is all I am, is all I know, it is all I do well.
It is all I have (and I
have more of it than I know what to do).

I soft-pedal it,
hold it just so,
traipse around with it
until my wrathful oath feels
validated. Like
a militant raising hell
before dissenting voices, flowered in copper-tinted bruises: I

"am too young to have seen it all"; do
"not have the tenor to claim"; it
"isn't wise to carry this burden"; so
"foul it twists my features like a bunched-up cloth"; it
"is shriller than it needs be"; feels

"unearned" — and derisively, they would tell us real
fury isn't reserved for the likes of you and I.

But girl, we've barely weathered all our storms: let guess
those who'd confine you
to categories that do you no justice. Could
you live with yourself if you did not have your say?
All these bruises I've
burgeoned, are just the occupational hazard, a
pitfall poets suffer when they answer to their Call.

We daughters, we start gathering up our flung pearls in infancy. It's
actually rather easy,
we forget how cruel it is if we do it enough.
And when we are handed the strand to
thread it all back together, do
up the delicate end around our choking throats like so, it
almost seems worth it, keeping it all in.

Truly: I look like a lady, this noose of nacre a
prize for my composure, my indignity sequestered to its cell.
And if it's
sometimes a little too easy
to forget the price other sisters have gone through — enough
to buy you the right to your open truth —, easy to
want to look the other way: do

not be greatly grieved about it.
You've barely weathered all your storms, and
you have only just begun. Stay
the hand on your displeasure, let it all stay put.
Soft-pedal it, hold it just so. It's
an exercise, endurance art, occupational hazard, the
thing that will Make you: and those idiot men would call you theatrical.

iv.

Everything we want is a
dream, unlikely as a miracle.

Everything I do that
shrieks of smallness, knocks
on doors with hinges bigger than me.
They swing in and they pivot out,
I have to move and dance around them. There
is a key here, as cryptic as is
unrelenting. Everything we want, a
concession with a charge.

Every time I spread and
give this hope a little wingspan, there
is no wind, strong enough, is
no earth soft enough to cushion it. A
concession with a charge
is too tedious to sustain, a
loud enough silence, is nearly always very
tedious, its wingspan much too large.
Every time I reach, I feel the promise, feel the charge.
Every time it's safe — but then again how long for?

Everywhere a graze, a
suggestive whisper of a word.
I'd give you my whole essence, or
at the very least allow a
little bashful touch.
Hold the promise near, or
let us be once and for all: a
promise given its bit
must be left alone, or of
course be paid for, always in moon-blood.

v.


And I will admit that I
hasten to condone my lapses before I am
even fully aware of your
displeasure: but have you forgotten? I am an opus
of contradictions that I
no longer bother to course correct: I am

your heel of Achilles, I am your
one flaw, I am that torment you have made valuable.

And I will acknowledge (the
latter a testament to my renewed good faith) that pure
pinwheel of interlocked claptrap and gold
I dole out. I curse you plentifully, even as you croon *"baby, baby"*.

And I do agree that
of the two of us, it is always your composure that melts,
hardened film of oil to
the scorching, thankless flame. A
crux you've come to relish, sigh to constant shriek.

And I could be more gentle; I
know that you are any port, and I am the storm, the turn
I can no longer afford to miss. And
I could be more gentle: but am I thankless, and do I burn.

And readily, readily, I will admit: I do
prod the soreness that need not
be prodded. But have you forgotten? I think
of you after I've tended to my own: I
am your heel of Achilles, I am that aftermath you underestimate,
I am the pinwheel of your
nightmares, and you think I am greater than great.
Tragic, yes — but that is none of my actual concern.

vi.

Wake from torpor, coughing ash,
sink hypnagogically, chewing ash.

It will not own you,
this hunger you prod and poke,

you prod and
sometimes stir.

You are withering made flesh.
You are bone, slivered bone.

Choke the flood that threatens there;
elegant tilt, winning disposition is

everything. The rest: means nothing.
Choke the flood and hold it there.

Brittle limbs will wear you out,
but you will be made an example of.

"She is transcendence itself!", despite the
prodded hunger, and the coughed and chewed up ash.

Claw the clawing ache, free the "it" from the "I",
swing from the torpor until again you rise.

You are nothing special to begin with.
A notch in a bigger pattern: "oh my!

How they ravage their psyches, how they rake their souls red!"
We spill out like pungent roe, like interlocking strands of greasy hair.

Erstwhile nourishing, the craving doesn't cease, only transfers: and
other vices breeze in, further bind the "it" and the "I".

Lavish, careen, luxuriate it away — but take care that you do not eat.
Regale yourself with your fellows, feast on the lust-laced contempt
of men,

embrace the tenets of your self-servitude like
so, and one day you might just cough and chew on air.

vii.

Saddled betwixt a
having of the cake
and the cleaning of

my mouth with soap

I corral my composure, ere a
steady envy marks the wedding
of the hollow thud and the vociferous ring,

of a
ghastly daydream, where ashes turn to gold
and I gather them around me: never filled, always filling.

## LONG SIMMER

Look into the light
Really, really look into the light
See that it's just tricks and shadows
Let that realization change you slowly

Give up your pipe dreams
Let go the razor blades
Trade your disaffected youth
For a semblance of adulthood

You've managed the pretense
Now pursue it to its end
Cut off your phone lines
And throw away your clothes

Shapeshift your face, your hair
Look like anyone else
Latch onto their sense of worth
Superpose it with yours

Hope this fancy sticks
Lose Her, then find God again
Make Her laugh, laugh at yourself
Quit your job, then change your name

Toss out your unread books
Jump out of cars, dance into traffic
Stand on corners and scream at the sky
Go ride the waves, ride them all the way

Win the lottery, better buy a boat
Abandon your loved ones
Shred the visa you were waiting for
You're not going to be there

Choose the pain, always the pain
Choose to turn yourself in
You are a caricature
Let them see the swindler behind the smile

Survive a zombie apocalypse
Befriend the oldest ghost
Follow cats down alleyways
Pat yourself on the back, stunner

Swallow the pills, swallow some more
Drown yourself in music
Hand over your tired thoughts
Swirl your finger in your numbness broth

Talk to your dead grandmother
Remember to bankrupt yourself
Spend your very last penny
On art you barely like

Be him, be Orpheus all the way
Look where they said not to
Upend the manner in which
You've been contemplating your inadequacies

Listen to the voices
Tell them "give me a minute"
Try to break your wrist again
Then hug yourself to sleep

Go on long and happy trips
Shout yourself into submission
Spiral like a spinning top
Find new places to live

Kill your little sister
Try to hang your shelves
Be the balance-beam
You've been revering in others

Shatter hollow promises
Admit you are a child
Let your actions speak for you
Then let them loose again

Unleash your inner optimist
Then chuck her in a box
Call yourself by your old name
Let it go to fun and hell

Decide not to wake up
Take pleasure in your apathy
And: favor the long goodbye at
The end of that crooked road

## HOW DOES SHE TALK?

Steady eyes I used to have steady soul steady head, my feet, steady;
I still have steady hands, alas my hands, they are still steady.

The rest: they split ways this and that, ran away with my composure and my clarity,
Did away with saneness and faith, but these fingers, always steady.

I have the artist's hand, hand that bends and curves, searches for purity,
The sublime line: that tracing that redresses all that wasn't steady.

I like clean lines, make it pretty, make it red raw, make it count.
Notch the directory where all things come together, come steady.

Blades and pencils, paintbrushes and razors, graphites and broken glass, ink markers;
Pressure obliterates from the soul, in bursts of steady.

It's faster than talking, faster than relief, won't requite tithes
On days and days that are all but steady:

On days when heart is haywire and air chokes out light, and sound
Totters and dies in your cochlea, soft and steady;

Days when sun hurts eyes but you draw the line and at last you can see;

Rush and rush endorphins, and you go steady.

How else, how else do you talk, how else do you create the world if not the line,
Straight narrow down the canvas, dash-firm and steady;

How else do you utter the unutterable if not the line,
Slate streaked red with crisscross, patterned and steady?

Subdue the wrist, inflect the hand, flood intention into your magnum opus:
Let the instrument speak you into Being, keep you steady.

# RED AND WHITE DON'T RUN TOGETHER

Year to year, a notion clashes against itself
against a world of notions.
I am Red, I am Crimson Crimson
Vermilion with anger
afire with despair when

will I stop being disappointed when those promises don't live up?

I would like a son
teach him what my men never learned.
I would like a son
teach him what my men should have understood.
I would like a son
teach him fingernails more than graze, they nick the
Skin doesn't weather the bruises it merely osmoses the
Pain is the yardstick we women are given from
Birth is the only fresh slate we are granted:

to undo the messes before they are made
to blot out the messes before they are indelible
Red breathing into White
both streaked with the other one's ghost.

I would like a son

continue here
what I was never able to finish:
but learned cynics never make great teachers.

Year to year, she puts down the mantle
takes it up again
from the tips of her fingers
sometimes
in staggered bursts of idealism.

Year to year, she says
*this one has broken me open yet again*
*scraped yet another layer from me.*
And still, she'd like a son
she'd like her faith to be rewarded
because hasn't she earned that by now
because hasn't she done enough lurching and wavering
and starting and swaying?
Hasn't she?

Year to year
she flits her Red rawness away like it's a fly
but it's an albatross she hasn't named for what it is
a swinging weight
couldn't bat it off, couldn't bat it away if she tried

because it's never that simple:
learned masochists never make great dreamers.

I fear I'll have a son
who'll tear another girl apart
with practiced, learned ease
with sanctioned, licensed cruelty.

These woods are full of these
and my feet have ambled their share
and I am Scarlet from it, scored Red to the creases in my joints.

Give me the daughter, then

I might not waste the magic on my fingertips just yet, just yet.
Give her to me fluid and supple
I might just make her the miscreant I became too late.
Give her to me wilder than I was, Incarnadine
I might have to lose her along the way so that she can
Free herself from the acceptance of this world's
Hindrance is a friend she'll come to know too
"Well enough" will often have to do

even when she wants only to scream
and she will be brave enough
to endure that
because don't we all, in the end
don't all of us women, at one point?

Maybe then I won't mind so much
maybe then it wouldn't matter:
that learned heartbreak makes for shitty mothers.

But year to year, truth tolls like howling bells
the sound it makes, a chafing only I can hear.

I don't want children.

Because this life, it always told me
Red and White don't run together.

# FALDERAL

    hand-wringer of the day    how to get out of a chinese finger trap: you don't pull, obviously (and what does that teach you about going against your instincts when something vital is on the line?)    just one of many puzzles i've been stuffing my head with since birth    solved rubik's cubes in theory but once they're in these hands    it's spinning hours and misspent days from then on thousand piece puzzles don't faze me, so how come this one did

    i say spin it this way and that    but when you tried to kill yourself, you weren't spinning so well were you    it felt much more monopoly-esque: roll the dice, do what it tells you    the other time it was like trying to make a word out of mismatched scrabble squares: ok so there's the pain    here there's a little turbulence    with this one you could spell tenacity    if you were so inclined    this one looks like trauma    that one, like dead-eyed cynicism    put all these bone-white squares together, you've got perhaps the so-called easy way out    why not why not, i say

    what was the question, how to get out    no, wasn't it: why trap your fingers in the first place    why induce the things you know will induce calamity, quick and categorical    like all those times you    jumped rope barefoot and persisted even as it cracked your bare calves played jenga under glaring lights flipped mikado sticks under the influence of mania and rage tackled poker menteur with seasoned liars    answer: because you like things that can make you laugh and you laugh best when you are scared

    it's like relative minors of a major scale kins from same-same stock but curiously inverted     i've been told i should surrender Perfection     i've seen her     that one's a pretty pretty talker     i've been told i should be looking outward     feel so selfish     how many times have i said i     but i cannot look past my too-tall thicket     is that something i should be saying aloud anyway the finger trap     back to the finger trap     recap: what did you learn today     i haven't been myself in a while     but i could have told you that

    don't hug me i'm going to cry     no really don't hug me     don't touch me don't touch me     first my hair, which you seem unable not to rake through

    then my skin caressed and complimented for its pulling blackness     but that is a story not for today     today i want the aforementioned hush for its own sake     not for some higher purpose     not out of a sense of collective justice (is that something i should be saying aloud)     a nacreous bubble     i am

    can contain it all but if you so much as thumb-graze my surface     i will puncture and it won't be pretty     i operate this feeling     like

    playing operation with bated breath     counting on that honk that'll advertise my failure for all to hear

    careful with that one     it's a tongue full of vinegar     all you'll be getting from there     wisdom says deal with it, talk about it, forgive yourself     but stay away from Guilt put her in a corner with that bitch Perfection     Guilt is like gum     step on it once, it's sticky steps from here on out     and i like to kiss the curbs

    sculpt your intentions around what you are trying to say — what *are* you trying to say what is wrong with you all of a sudden     you're so good with words     why can't you just say it *i feel like dying*     why must you take the metaphorical avenues and tricky byways just to call a thing a thing

    because your memory is short leash     don't you remember what happened the last time you went on this ride     actually i haven't i'm just taking break i'm just taking it easy on the agony wagon

    you haven't learned a thing     have dillied and dallied     have flimmed and flammed and learned nothing     the trick is to not try so hard after all the trick to it is

    pinch your fingers together, make them touch     hope the stiffness folds and one of them catches free     least that's what every film you've seen says will work     if all else fails you could still enjoy that useless pull-pull stretching     it feels like pulling taffy     you saw that once when you went to the carnival     as a child     and you've been craving sugar since

## III. HOLD THE WAVE

## HOLDING WATER

I am a fish in your sea
yours is a dusky one

treasure chests of whorls and eddies
come at me from all sides

yet, you wouldn't know that
you think yourself a flat surface

uninteresting
unicolored

you are unique-
ly colored

flat surfaces couldn't have broken me so
pieces, my pieces, floating in all corners of your ocean

soggy, wrinkled, color bled out like ink-apposed notes
I am a fish in your sea

and you are like water

hold my fingers, fan them out
you are like holding water.

## ECHOES, AFTERTHOUGHTS

Technicolor childhood, stop motion fun
Pain tastes like salt, smells like rain, looks like sea
Watercolor coming of age, echoes of a gun
Hurts me like a fire that will not sear
Yet to ring out, pressed against your temple
No. It pains like echoes, afterthoughts, quails
Go, give way to your nostalgia, be gentle
Like a waif, pretend you are not there
I've forgotten how to comfort other people
I'm an animal, I seldom respond to the Call
I come on too strong, or else I get feeble
Somewhere along the way, I'll learn to have it all

## ANHEDONIS, ANHEDONIA

I am tired of worrying my youth away, I am tired of being worried, I am tired
You want to hold on to it, that certain lightness of being
You said child, child: once it goes, never comes your way again

Simone says "ain't nobody perfect 'cause ain't nobody free"
Couldn't be perfect, lightness forbid, could never be free
I am tired of worrying my youth away, I am tired of being worried, I am tired

Only have my words, warping the Eye turned toward the world
Yearn to reach those masterful heights, paralyzed by victory
You said child, child: once it goes, never comes your way again

No lessons, just losses, walk long tunnels, don't see their end
I shut these titillations away in my sanded wooden drawers
I am tired of worrying my youth away, I am tired of being worried, I am tired

But sometimes the weight, it jams and they flicker out
Tendrils reaching reaching touching invasive
You said child, child: once it goes, never comes your way again

So girl: wash the sunshine off your skin
Blinkered lights, wintered souls at dawn
I am tired of worrying my youth away, I am tired of being worried, I am tired
You said child, child: once it goes, never comes your way again

## HOTHOUSE FLOWER

*let us go down there then*
*taste the sound of your*
*favorite pretext and give it*
*ready-made it's not your fault*
*i know you bruise so easily*
*barely brushed*
*barely listened*
*hardly heeded*
*it's a shield waved in false anguish*
*the tragedy whispered under fluttered eyelashes*
*the unspoken pretext swimming in the lake of your theatrics*
*you bruise so easily*
*let us go down there then*
*touch it see how it sounds*
*you bruise so easily*
*so easily gives leave to slice and harm with forlorn tease*
*i cannot have not the right to point out your hardness*
*but when did you last call your mother*
*let us all go down there*
*funnysorry sights*
*won't we all have monstrous things to say*

My fault. I remember, I forget
You never fail to remind me

How I have harmed you, how you have harmed me
"But if you got wiser, I would not, would never"
"But you kept going"
"But I should have reached back"
I should have bet on that tenacity of yours
That snakes its way into my conscience
And always finds me in the end
And can I say: I have really tried and set sails.
Let us not go there, let us not prod the hull of that boat
We shall sway, and therein lies only reproach and that mouthful of
Bland nostalgia
I haven't called, won't answer letters
Won't even give the courtesy of assent
Because I bruise so easily
And everything is out of touch, so let us not go there
Therein lies sadness, sometimes, melancholy, even, that panic, stale and pedestrian
But pedestrian is good enough, pedestrian is better than fury, more intricate than fury

## PAPER TIGER MAN


*not just twelve / nearly thirteen /* i tell the man / who leans down / whispers in the crook of my shoulder / he has laughter and beer / on his tongue / and something else / something heavy / and possibly harmful / *funny / you barely even look twelve to me / you ever wonder / what your life will be like / when you're my age /* again he laughs / places a welted hand / on my bare shoulder / *then again i suppose / it's too early for you / to start thinking about the end /* i look him up and down / *actually monsieur / no / been having existential crises / since i could string words / together /* he leans closer / the others / they give him a wide berth / joyless tourists / slouched on splintering benches / i am no less morose / i am a spot of grey / ashen composure / under a clouded tuesday dawn / clouded dawn / over this slate-colored area / of the saint-exupéry gare de lyon / the man / of the beer-and-laughter breath / sidles nearer / he has seen my distracted chaperone / relinquish his vigilance for a cup of coffee / nearby / he has seen the father of three on my right / too embarrassed to intervene / not enough / to do anything about it / he has seen the woman / whose eyes scream / *get out / vas-t'en / laisse-la tranquille /* he has seen her look / away / he has seen / open dejection / homesickness on my face / and he has mistaken it / for vulnerability

i narrow sneering eyes / i gather my things to leave / he says / *you shouldn't be so scared of people /* but what does he know / i am not scared of anything / of anyone / have never been scared / tussle with fear / chew it out for breakfast / what does he know / i am just tired / i am just tired already /

not yet a woman / not even yet a teenager / and already tired / and well-acquainted with strangers / whose breaths reek of beer / or laughter / or violence / or deception / or apologies / or all the above / it's been one year / since i've been catcalled through a car window / two / since i've been flirted with by a man thrice my age / four / since i've felt aflame with discomfort at a wandering touch / eight / since a stray remark i couldn't yet pinpoint for its inappropriateness / and more and more / and i just don't have time for this / it's only tuesday / and it's dawn / and i'm going to be jet-lagged / and i miss my parents / and the chaperone shouldn't have gone / to chase a cup of coffee / and i want my seat by the window / so i can glaze my weary eyes / over the landscape / and who is he to tell me / how i should feel / when i don't know for myself / half the time / anymore / *you shouldn't be so scared / i only want to talk / haven't you ever been bored?*

but he is not wrong / he has merely seen the future / i am not scared / but i will be / i will know fear / will feel for it / will tentatively tread it / will sink my tired feet in it / will have it run up my legs / like molasses left to congeal / i will see into the souls of men / not the waning beauty / that i look upon now / at twelve-nearly-thirteen-years-old / but the otherness / that terrible notion / of potential / of suggestions of terror / of the power to wield unimaginable damage / and i will wish i couldn't / will wish i couldn't see / will wish my wisdom was misplaced / my misgivings disproportionate / i will wish i was / but never ever / will i ever / be wrong

but what matters right now / right this moment / under a clouded tuesday dawn / over the slate-colored area / of the saint-exupéry gare de lyon / is that this still-hungover man / is wrong / i do not cave to fear / and perhaps he can sense it too / why else / would he have singled me / out of all the joyless tourists / slouched on splintering benches / heartbroken homesick jet-lagged / hoping for windows and landscapes / out of which to rest / weary foreheads and gazes

and then at last / all of a sudden / i can see it after all / beyond the hirsute stubble / and the ebbing drunkenness / and the brusque marseille cadence / and the mean curl of the mouth / and the mismatched cufflinks / and the welts on the gnarled hands / and the knuckle clenching the train ticket / and the laughter and the beer / broken sad lonely / wanting to connect with someone / anyone / just to know he is alive / to know he has shape and weight / even if it means accosting / a twelve-nearly-thirteen year old / who has had ample time / to lose her own sense / of shape and weight / or / perhaps i am being kind / once again allowing / a broken man's brokenness / to infringe upon my own / a choice i'll come to exercise / like a reflex by the time / i am thirteen / actually thirteen / but under this clouded tuesday dawn / over the slate-colored area / of the saint-exupéry gare de lyon / it is not fear written / on this small face / it is insolence / laced with skepticism / the mask i will learn to wear / over the years / in lieu of the bawling rabid fear / *now that we've established / that i am not scared / and that you are bored / what do you want / to talk about?*

# I TOOK A STROLL WHILE COMING DOWN

And got lost wandering in the photography section of the museum
*Scenes from Brazzaville circa 1955*
I couldn't focus on how beautifully they challenged notions of glamor
Displayed in a space that valued nothing of that culture
All I could do was dully drift, sidestep each picture, lean into it and stare
That man is dead now
And this one
And this one
And this one too — unless he was particularly prudent and took care not to play with fire
In that case maybe he's a really old man by now, chilling on his deathbed waiting for the end
So I stand corrected. This man isn't dead yet
He's more likely die-ing. Which rings a little different
To be fair

There's a section on West African art
Ghana, Ghana, Ghana again, Ivory Coast ornaments
Pottery pieces from Mali
Red ochre and milky amber
I look for my mother's country
A lady nearby asks if I am alright — oh look, I am now sobbing
I say
I can't find Senegal anywhere on this gigantic map

And she takes it to mean anguish
I don't say
Suddenly feels like I am near a boat
Or rather in one
Water soaking down the flooding ramparts
And sinking me with it
This thing is wearing off and I am going to be sick
I don't say no don't worry I'm not really crying
In fact I feel like laughing
But I won't do that else I'll scare you more than I just did

I ambled into the African cloth installment
Dark room, four glass walls lit from within
I sat, a swaying vessel
And thought of my grandmothers
In their multicolored wax prints, headwraps draped and perched
Like a kaleidoscopic song
Brighter than the sun
This glass, it does not do these cloths justice
They don't look so dull cascading from knees onto floor in pretty bundles
Or maybe color is leaking from my eyelids
I, too, am lit from within
And it is spilling out, outward
If I heave all this water overboard
I might salvage this plummeting boat
I should go home
If I stop crying I'm going to laugh
And it feels woefully inappropriate
No one should laugh alone

# UNDERCLOUD

It occurred to me
that when you ask me obvious questions,
you may simply be wanting to hear me talk;
like when I let grip loosen on mug handle,
knowing it will fall,
just so I can hear the scintillation,
that shatter-shatter.
Elephantine silences are greedy;
I imagine you must be yearning for the modest
cadences of our conversations,
the sort of thing you get to missing
idly,
even though you shouldn't.

> Sunshine, it chases me and I take it personally; at its mercy on this bed, it means rolling away from the inevitable graze of it, slow slither of garter snake onto open skin. I close blinds, arch my neck, contort contort contort till I am *angle-droit*, till I start to think that migrating rooms would take less effort. I want to scream, but you can't argue with the sun, you can't argue with something bigger than yourself, though you have certainly tried. I am reminded of the finger, that one you wouldn't keep off my thigh: even when I pushed it bounced back and all I could do was sigh. It occurred to me that when you make contact with my skin, you

may simply be wanting to get closer than I'll allow. I am flexible, but I haven't allowed you much.

And like the shatter-shatter chases the slip of the mug,
like comfortable cadences of tired-but-shared stories,
so, too, do I miss you.
But in a hopeful way,
in a way that is sometimes garish
(or endearing if let be, if I
stop trying so hard to be so cool all the time),
in a way that could make me like summer again
and hate the sun a little, just a little less.

## ALL THIS MESS, IT DOESN'T LEAVE YOU WHEN YOU GO

record skates on needle, needle pesters faulty groove
skipping, one would say, but in reality is not
hasn't halted. *don't you call me static motion*
linearity of sound has simply exited the chat
veered off by a needle that will not let up or course correct

this room is haunted, squinting, failing string lights crawled like vines
along its walls. here a dazzle flicker, there an inky halo, emptied eye
sockets after plucked out eyeballs

going in-out like a taunt

sound and light in tandem, trading their own versions of silence — the
blinking, the skipped music
it leaves spaces for the rest to dip the toe

it's like that old madness, the one that churns awareness out of streams of
thought
rearranges them like an artful villanelle
blistered sounds made to make sense

lost a year of life's worth of words in this room
records ruined one after the other
for the sake of a needle I would not change

this record player desecrating my loves
in the backdrop of all else breaking apart
still felt far from trivial

never learned to let go of iotas

when the ceiling chipped overhead it was scraped off with a blade
when the hinges stopped their nimble swinging they were twisted, cast off
when the parquet, it was cracked, we slathered wax over the gashes
bent and buckled bones mending craters in the wallpaper
patched the caulked window when it lift and lifted
cracked and cracked the gathering ice

never yet a home, never yet a comfort
but always tended to
the way this here soul never was

now, this
a sting of lights, a replaceable vinyl
are as ridiculous as ridiculous gets

iotas, of course, but cherished ones

those blinking bulbs
that stuttering music
those hollow repairs
it says ruination, spells collapse
still, it's not the worse it has seen
this room it cannot let itself go while
something weightier commands the center

I ate a cyclone, thinking its wild and frenzied cycles might alleviate my staticity. instead the dust has been unsettled on encroached and static things

when I raised this bookshelf from the ground up, I was shedding homesick tears
over there, I curved, after months of frozen sorrow

cradled a cantankerous kitten where the poster curls up slowly
that there corner houses many a nameless secret
this wine-colored rug has soaked more than its share of blood
phantom howling paces all corners of this space

all this mess, it doesn't leave you when you go
probably, I should have stopped the patching up when it crumbled
these things were never really threatened
something weightier pulls the center

it says:
find your own language
make your grief sing
make it make sense
turn it over
until you can hear again
until the words come to you easy(er)
*this & this happened. wouldn't recommend it*

and when you've braced enough, lift that needle, unplug those lights, and please leave this goddamn room.

## SOMETIMES YOU GET THE BEAR

I'd sit on the edge of somnolence and watch Opportunity
come to me fast, fast, but I'd be ready.
First on the train gets the ride,
that how it goes?
I'd ruffle sleep's heavy powder from my shoulders;
was never much of a sleeper;
would wait on Expectation the way
countertops welcome the drip-drip of an overflowing glass
held by jittery hands:
inevitable, but not that dramatic after all.

I'm not sure if you know,
I used to thumb my nose at Disappointment,
wasn't for me,
never felt that.
Shrouded inner child, when did you stop shadowing me?
Where did the hour go?

The things we used to believe in are plenty and strange, namely that:
if we slept sideways on a deck, a single ant could crawl into an ear and undo our thoughts
licking dirty envelopes with slit tongues could seed a small family of roaches in our mouths

swallowed seeds would burst and scale up, abdomen through chest, and grow from our heads
swimming past the sunline from the shore, we'd grow scales and at last meet the vampire squid
if matches were lit after sundown, we could summon the devil and gamble with his cronies
a needle touched at twilight could bring a person, any person, back to life.
Now: you still howl in my chest, little girl, and I am tone deaf, I am tone deaf.

I'm not sure if you know.

I'm selling you something
utterly fabricated,
utterly false,
illusory,
pinpricked here and there
and made flawless to satisfy the appearances I roam through;
but grifter, grifter, your words, my grain of salt.

And we always wanted something we could call our own,
adulthood, trite and glorified,
delivered onto our puny feet —
who knew it would involve so much of being wary,
so much of being worried all the time?

I don't want to be a promise,
a being made of potentials
and splendor yet to come.
I want to be whole, nine years old, like you:
I just want to be.

And I want that wholeness to claim me,
to take me under, to pare away at me
until I am red open and alive and
full of flaws again.
Perfection is overrated,
I see this now.

Finish something, any one thing, everyday.
You can't want everything,
no, you can't want everything.
Stop being a sourpuss, faultfinder;
you are better than that,
better than that, which I am not sure you know.

## HOW YOU WRITE A TALL TALE

been bragging about holding water
been talking smack about coughing and chewing ash
been boasting about all the cyclones i ate
they say all boats rise
but mine must not have gotten the message
riddled with holes i made when i was bored
out of all my senses
all i do is sink
and still i find it in myself: to be shocked

but shock is a plateau
the most predictable of tediums
i've been chasing shaky grounds lately
after it left me nothing could upend my life
after i uprooted my life nothing could make me shudder
after the shuddering ghost came to visit, dragging fingers on the tinny
wind chimes tugging on the tips of my hair strands tugging on my toes in
time to music: nothing could make my ear sing

so i went to sea instead

i was called bluebeard in a past life, resisted paper tiger men, wrestled
red into white like the brave little tailor swatting giants with a lie

that mythology, i dreamt and authored it, rollicked in it rage-ful and frenzy-ful, the story changing at every swirl and tide: black girl crazy girl drifter mermaid sailor holding waves, pantagruelic exaggerations

once i sailed from dakar to chicago by the strength of my certitude, buffeted by purpled currents i was determined to elude, john henry making waves

i spent the month of august, my eyes picked apart piecemeal, in fits and starts, to distract from the picking apart of my grey matter

instead i ended up with multitude-eyes and multitude-vision, impossible to escape and to keep from seeing better; argus panoptes would have been impressed

lost three, five years, ten years lying in bed, letting life wash over me, letting guitar and piano gather dust, pencils stay sharpened, watching films and watching my life, like a film, sail by

and they say: if you teach yourself to stand taller than you are, ground your toes into the sand even when your beanstalk sways, they'll never mistake you for icarus again

even at the cost of honesty, even at the cost of vulnerable — fuck vulnerable, hasn't done anything for you in this life

but you can only go so far until you come to land again

and again, eventually, you will have to walk — sealegs, vertigo, motion sickness be damned

so why don't you?

you have to start somewhere
this is not a roadmap
a resolution
or an ironclad promise
it's just a start, just a start
laid out timid on the page

put it away for a while and come back to it when
and only when

the water: it will always be there when you again need to kiss shores and
sail away

so claim this notion
gently
pretend it's a new pair of shoes you're breaking in
seven-league boots slick-shiny, so taut it bends your toes inward
so taut you feel leather on pink bones with every leap
walk around with it, take it around the block, see
how it feels
unnatural, yes, but is it something
you could get used to?

that's the first, real honest question
you have asked yourself of late
and when you pen it, it may just
— hear me out:
help you curb that wave.

## ACKNOWLEDGMENTS

Acknowledgement is given to the following literary journals and magazines, in which these poems have been published.

*8 Poems*, "all this mess, it doesn't leave you when you go"
*Anti-Heroin Chic*, "Hothouse Flower"
*Blood Orange*, "I Have Faith In Birds"
*Boston Accent Lit*, "Sometimes You Get The Bear"
*Capsule Stories*, "Undercloud"
*Confessionalist Zine*, "In-Out"
*Crack the Spine*, "Late Bloomer"
*Déraciné Magazine*, "The Thrill," "So You've Got a Dinner Party," "Long Simmer," "Echoes, Afterthoughts"
*Doghouse Press*, "Bald Eyes"
*Dream Pop Journal*, "Kintsugi of Sorts"
*Feminine Collective*, "Very Specific Phobias"
*Figure 1*, "Holding Water"
*Gone Lawn*, "Paper Tiger Man"
*Ligeia*, "Iotas"
*Moonchild Magazine*, "Falderal"
*Night Music Journal*, "Hammers"
*Porridge Mag*, "Fortune Favors"
*RIC Journal*, "Succors," "How Does She Talk?"
*Rogue Agent*, "Hills to Die On"

*South Broadway Ghost Society,* "And You Will Call Me Bluebeard"
*Tenderness Lit,* "How You Write A Tall Tale"
*TERSE. Journal,* "Anhedonis, Anhedonia"
*Variant Lit,* "Icarus Bystander"
*Willawaw Journal* "I Took A Stroll While Coming Down"

## ABOUT THE AUTHOR

Aïcha Martine Thiam is a trilingual and multicultural writer, musician and artist who goes where the waves take her. She might have been a kraken in a past life. She's an Editor at *Reckoning*, Editor-in-Chief, Producer and Creative Director of *The Nasiona*, and has been nominated for Best of the Net, The Best Small Fictions and The Pushcart Prize. Her collection *AT SEA* was shortlisted for the 2019 *Kingdoms in the Wild* Poetry Prize. @Maelllstrom/www.amartine.com.

## ALSO BY CLASH BOOKS

**WATERFALL GIRLS**
Kimberly White

**BURIALS**
Jessica Drake-Thomas

**AN EXHALATION OF DEAD THINGS**
Savannah Slone

**I'M FROM NOWHERE**
Lindsay Lerman

**NAKED**
Joel Amat Güell

**REGRET OR SOMETHING MORE ANIMAL**
Heather Bell

**ALL THE PLACES I WISH I DIED**
Crystal Stone

**THE SMALLEST OF BONES**
Holly Lyn Wallrath

**PAPI DOESN'T LOVE ME NO MORE**
Anna Suarez

**CENOTE CITY**
Monique Quintana

**WE PUT THE LIT IN LITERARY**

CLASHBOOKS.COM

**TWITTER**

IG

FB

@clashbooks

**Email**

clashmediabooks@gmail.com

www.ingramcontent.com/pod-product-compliance
Lightning Source LLC
Chambersburg PA
CBHW022013120526
44592CB00034B/799